# Cat Tales Family Album

## Photos by
## Harry W. Freese

My name is Snuffy McFriskie and this is my family photo album.

My twin sister Sniffy and me (Snuffy).

The photographs on the following pages were taken by the renowned animal photographer Harry Whittier Freese. They represent one of the earliest methods of photographing animals without the use of drugs, wires, braces, or any other form of physical restraint. Freese was able to successfully photograph animals poised in humorous situations without inflicting any pain or discomfort.

ISBN 0-89542-477-0 225

Copyright © MCMLXXIX by Ideals Publishing Corporation
All rights reserved
Printed and bound in the United States of America
Published simultaneously in Canada

Published by Ideals Publishing Corporation
11315 Watertown Plank Road
Milwaukee, Wisconsin 53226

**Editorial Director,** James Kuse
**Managing Editor,** Ralph Luedtke
**Production Editor/Manager,** Richard Lawson
**Photographic Editor,** Gerald Koser
**Copy Editor,** Sharon Style

**Designed by** Beverly Rae Wiersum

**Me, Sniffy, and our friends, Chester and Ozzie went sledding in January.
(I didn't make it down the hill.)**

**We had a big snowball fight. (I lost.)**

**Tom sent cousin Curly Catfield a valentine love letter and a serenade...**

**...while Buffy used other ways to court her.**

**Buffy won. A purrrrfect pair (Curly and Buffy).**

**We had a tough time flying our kite on a windy March day.**

**Sniffy gathered eggs to dye for Easter . . .**

**. . . while I was caught lying down on the job.**

**April showers . . .**

... bring May flowers.

**Fluffy's Mother's Day present was helping Mom clean.**

**Later, Mom had to clean up Fluffy.**

**Fluffy sure was tired that night.**

**Curly and Buffy decided to tie the knot.**

Minister Meow performed the ceremony.

For the honeymoon they went to the Catskill Mountains.

**Sniffy and I sneaked off from school to go fishing.**

**Catfish! (I never was very good at fishing.)**

**For Sniffy's and my birthday we went to the amusement park . . .**

**. . . and rode on the Catastrophic Coaster Ride.**

**On the Fourth of July Grand-paw led the parade...**

**...and Sniffy marched to the beat.**

**In the annual Balloon Races the Three Little Kittens (the ones who lost their mittens) came in second.**

Sniffy and I came in first.

At the races the vendor sold a lot of our favorite dessert.

At our family picnic . . .

. . . we had a tug-of-war: the Catfields against the McFriskies.

I snapped this shot of my brother Hairy Jr. after his baseball game.

We all caught a quick catnap (Fluffy, Sniffy, and me).

**Then we had to go back to school.**

**Our second grade teacher was Miss La Furr.**

**After school we gathered chestnuts.**

**At our Halloween costume party everyone dressed up:**

Sniffy

Chester

Fanny

Buffy

Me

Ozzie

**In November we fulfilled our pet-riotic duty and voted.**

**For Thanksgiving dinner Sniffy peeled the potatoes...**

... while I was "rolling in dough."

**Fluffy took out the final product—pumpkitten pie.**

**Then the family shouted, "Bring on the turkey!"**

**Fluffy got stuck with the dishes.**

**At Christmas I baked cookies for Santa . . .**

**. . . but I was too tired to wait up for him on Christmas Eve.**

**Santa Claws.**

Santa emptied his pack.

On Christmas morning I discovered all the toys Santa left.

**I had a very merry Christmas.**

**I hope you liked my family album. Goodnight!**